Exquisite plant life thrives in a land of extremes.

CONTENTS

Lion Lake #2, Rocky Mountain National Park

"The Earth laughs in flowers."
— Ralph Waldo Emerson

FOREWORD

*O*f the more than 330 species of tundra plants found in Colorado, at least 180 have been located within Rocky Mountain National Park. The park is an exceptional resource, for such accessible richness and expanse of tundra are not found elsewhere in the United States outside of Alaska.

Many of these plants are grasses and sedges, but the array of flowering plants gives the tundra a beauty difficult to equal. This book includes the Rocky Mountain National Park region's more common and conspicuous alpine plants, the ones any visitor is likely to encounter on a stroll through this alpine world. A few inconspicuous species are included because of their ecological interest.

Alpine Wildflowers is a revised version of the original work by Beatrice E. Willard, Ph.D., and Chester Harris that first appeared in 1963. Now out of print, that book soon proved to be an important resource for students of the alpine tundra, and a successor became a priority. This work is organized by color to ease the search for species. The reader also may want to review the index in the back of the book to check other characteristics of the species. Many of the scientific names used here are those listed by William A. Weber in his *Rocky Mountain Flora* or his more recent *Colorado Flora: Western Slope*. They reflect considerable change in scientific nomenclature. Highly recommended for the reader who would like to learn more about alpine tundra natural history is the classic *Land Above the Trees* by Ann H. Zwinger and Beatrice E. Willard.

A word about visiting the tundra. Alpine plants possess many remarkable adaptations to survive in an extremely harsh world, but they cannot tolerate the repeated impact of human feet. Once impacted, tundra sites may take hundreds of years to recover. Popular visitor areas along Trail Ridge Road within Rocky Mountain National Park have been designated as Tundra Protection Areas. In these areas – Forest Canyon Overlook, Rock Cut, Gore Range Overlook and the Alpine Visitor Center – no foot traffic is allowed off the trails. However, off-trail travel is acceptable away from these congested areas.

When walking on the tundra, always consider the effects of your presence. Step on rocks where you can, and spread out your group to minimize impact. Avoid walking single file. In national parks, collecting is prohibited. It's also devastating to tundra plants. Rydbergia, for example, may use energy gathered through many difficult seasons to produce its first and only flower head.

Enjoying the alpine tundra always means paying attention to the weather. Summer lightning storms can swiftly sweep in to catch travelers far from protection, and snowstorms can occur any day of the year. Take along several layers of clothing so you can adapt to all conditions. Foul-weather gear is a must. Eye and skin protection also is important in this high-elevation world. Winds of 155 miles per hour have been recorded on Trail Ridge, so be sure to retreat in the face of approaching storms. Plan to return another day.

Introduction To Alpine Tundra Wildflowers

*A*top the mountains of Rocky Mountain National Park lies the vast, sublime alpine tundra. This region beyond where trees can grow appears at first glance to be a barren desert, but in fact, it contains a wealth of miniature plants. When examined closely, the tiniest plants appear exquisitely expressed with incredible flourish. Such magnificent beauty thrives amid the stressful forces of wind, frost, drought, intense sunlight and churning soil, all producing the ultimate juxtaposition in contrasts.

Nearly one third of Rocky Mountain National Park is carpeted with alpine tundra. Tundra, a word derived from the Russian language meaning land of no trees, is a label comparable to forest, desert or grassland. It refers to major ecosystems located above the limit of trees on mountains or beyond the limit where trees can grow in the Arctic and Antarctic regions of Alaska, Canada, Scandinavia, Siberia and Tierra del Fuego.

Alpine Tundra Through The Seasons

*I*n summer, myriad flowers bedeck the alpine tundra, splashing it with all colors of the spectrum for a few brief weeks. In the Rocky Mountains, yellows and blues are the most numerous. Summer is a wonderful time to visit the tundra. Dozens of plant species bloom in the tundra, compelling travelers to stoop for a better look – a delightful pastime that leads from discovery to discovery.

Among the tundra treasures are cushions of pink, fringe-petaled moss campion and white sandwort covering barren gravels and carpets of rosy dwarf clover flowing between the boulders. Hugging the ground are dense pads of alpine nailwort ornamented with tiny yellow-green flowers so perfectly formed that at first, they don't appear real. Sprinkled throughout are the white star clusters of rockjasmine and clumps of yellow alpine avens set in masses of fern-like leaves.

Spring is an even more thrilling time for discoveries. On most days, the sun's warmth rapidly melts snowdrifts and penetrates the soils deeply frozen by winter's cold. It only takes a few days of above-freezing temperatures before the delicate – but brilliant – magenta blossoms of alpine primrose, vivid-blue alpine forget-me-not and white candytuft burst forth at summer's return. Spring brings a daily transformation that reaffirms life's continuity from season to season.

For some tundra plants, this springtime moment of release occurs when deep winter snowdrifts thaw weeks after the emergence of the first alpine forget-me-not. But the snow buttercup is prepared to unfurl its glossy-yellow petals; it may push up through the thin edge of snowdrifts and flower before the snow departs.

Autumn brings golden hues to the alpine tundra.

Autumn, which comes early to the tundra, even by late July, brings a sense of relaxation following the exceedingly rapid and compressed activity of the foreshortened spring and summer. But fall is not without its visual treats, one of which is the appearance of the arctic gentian's long white urns adorned with dark-purple stripes. Blooming of these striking flowers heralds summer's end. Soon to follow is the turning of tiny leaves to autumn reds, golds and bronzes, giving the tundra its greatest displays of color. Most striking is the rich burgundy-red foliage of alpine avens, the most common plant in the park's tundra. When backlit by the sun, the leaves are reminiscent of light passing through a glass of vintage red wine.

Then one day, with little or no warning, this pageant of color is blanketed by the first winter snow. The storm may be either silent and gentle or boisterous and forceful. The white veil left behind may melt quickly and be followed by more of the still and warm days of autumn, or the snow may be reinforced with yet another and another snowfall, irretrievably bringing winter to the tundra for another year.

*O*nce in this desert-like land, travelers begin to distinguish the subtle differences of color and texture in the fabric of vegetation. These patterns indicate major plant community types.

Fellfields

The carpet-like fellfield is a highly unusual community. Adorned with bright flowers in the summer and strewn with rocks of all sizes, from sand to boulders, fellfields are found in dry, windswept sites along ridge crests. Swept by howling winds much of the year and perched where water evaporates quickly or drains away easily, fellfield habitats pose challenges to plant survival second only to deserts.

Fellfield plants respond to these environmental rigors by growing close to the ground in compact cushions and mats. This adaptation enables them to live within the boundary layer of the air and ground, a very shallow environment where the wind is calmer and the temperature much warmer than in the open air. Cushion and mat growth forms are found in fellfields throughout the world, attesting to the effectiveness of this adaptation.

The tiny leaves of fellfield plants permit little water loss to occur, and they are covered with hairs or wax that also reduce evaporation. These cushion and mat plants are anchored by long, strong taproots that extend deep into the rocks, sometimes reaching small pockets of water. The flowers of cushions and mats barely extend above the surface of the main plant body. Common fellfield plants are moss campion, dwarf clover, alpine sandwort, alpine nailwort, alpine phlox and mountain dryad.

Alpine Turfs

Large areas of tundra support tough, dense turfs. These gently undulating, lawn-like meadows are not covered by snow in winter. As a result, they have the longest growing season and possess the largest plant variety of any alpine community. Turfs are dominated by tiny, grass-like sedges distinguished by their triangular stems. The masses of shallow, fibrous roots of the sedges hold the deep, fine tundra soil and keep it from being eroded by the fierce winds and rain.

Turf communities are the most advanced, complex ecosystems in the alpine tundra. They come into being gradually as sedges and other erect plants slowly invade the cushions and mats of fellfields. As this invasion takes place, fellfield soils slowly incorporate more decaying plant material, making it possible for other erect plants to survive. The developing turf continues to grow and crowd out the cushion and mat plants. Characteristic flowers include Rydbergia, alplily, moss gentian, American bistort, greenleaf chiming bells and mountain candytuft. Also common in alpine turf areas are western yellow paintbrush.

Snowbeds

Especially interesting are snowbed communities found in depressions where snow accumulates all winter and remains long into summer. Plants living in snowbeds have a short growing season, but they are protected from the scouring winds and cold temperatures by insulating blankets of snow – as paradoxical as that may seem. Some 2 1/2 feet or more below snow surfaces, temperatures remain between 26 degrees and 28 degrees Fahrenheit, while air temperatures can be -16 degrees or lower. Snow buttercup and Sibbaldia (cloverleaf rose) are distinctive plants of these areas.

Wet Meadows

Dark-green, luxuriant wet meadows are highly conspicuous, occupying small, depressed areas. The source of their water is not obvious, for there are no streams, and these wet meadows are not necessarily growing beneath or downhill from snowbanks.

Most water that reaches wet meadows comes either in summer as rain or during the rest of the year as snow. A small amount may drain in from above. Once there, the water is frozen during cold seasons into masses of ice in the ground. Water also freezes to existing ice masses and enlarges them. In summer, these buried ice masses melt slowly – but not completely – to irrigate the wet meadows, even forming shallow pools behind terraces. Common plants in wet meadows are white marsh-marigold, queens crown, alpine lousewort and willows.

Gopher Gardens

In mid-summer, another distinctive community commonly seen is the gopher garden. There, concentrations of blue sky pilot and greenleaf chiming bells, yellow alpine avens, wine-red kings crown, white American bistort and tufts of alpine wheatgrass and purple reedgrass alternate with bare patches of gravel. These plants signal where pocket gophers have excavated the earth in search of roots. These colorful gardens last decades, then give way to cushion plants if the gophers do not plow the area again.

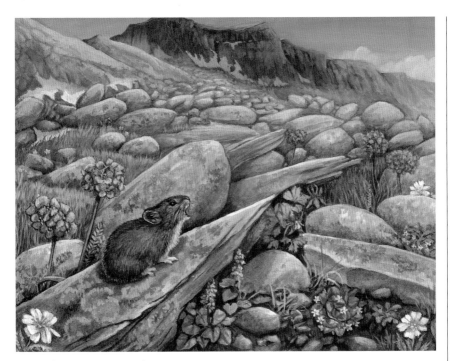

Rock And Gravel Areas

 Tucked into crevices among large boulders and seen on bare gravel are plants that do not compete well: big-rooted springbeauty, alpine sorrel, goldbloom saxifrage and dotted saxifrage. Shaded, sheltered rock ledges and the spaces beneath overhangs are the secret homes of alpine columbine and weakstem saxifrage.

Arctic Climate And
Rocky Mountain Alpine Weather

*T*ravel beyond treelimit into the alpine tundra is passage from one of Earth's major climates into another – from temperate climate into arctic climate. Arctic climate has several characteristics, most distinctive of which are winters five months or more in length and air temperatures never above freezing during winter months. Maximum air temperatures in winter rarely exceed 20 degrees F; in summer, temperatures rarely get above 65 degrees. In arctic climate regions, blizzards can occur during any season of the year.

A typical annual cycle of weather within the arctic climate region of Rocky Mountain National Park brings minimum temperatures of -35 degrees in January. This is much higher than the lows experienced in mountain valleys, which receive cold air drainage. The warmest temperature is 70 degrees in July, and there is an average of only 47 frost-free days each year. Winds of up to 201 miles per hour have been recorded on alpine summits. Average precipitation is 40 inches per year at the highest elevations, with 40 percent coming in spring, 35 percent from summer thundershowers and 25 percent from winter storms. More important, wind-blasted areas may retain only a few inches of snow.

Summer days are usually in the 50s to low 60s, and nights stay above freezing unless blizzards drop temperatures into the high 20s. Westerly winds blow most days, often to 45 miles per hour. Most summer days also include one or more thundershowers, a very important natural sprinkler system for the plant communities.

Autumn days may be either warm and windless or cold and snowy. Depending on the intensity of the storm and how much the weather warms afterward, all the snow may melt off during Indian summer or remain to begin the winter's accumulation.

Winter days can be sunny, but they are always cold. Winds often gale to more than 100 miles per hour. Frequent storms sweep in over the western states from the Gulf of Alaska and deposit most of their moisture to the west of the Rockies. Very little moisture remains in the air when it reaches Colorado, making the snow that falls quite dry. The winds extract moisture from vegetation and land, especially on the tundra and east slope of the Rockies. These winds redistribute snow into depressions and glacial cirques, where it accumulates to considerable depth and in some places, remains from one season to the next.

Spring in the tundra is quite a contrast to that in lower-elevation temperate climates. In the high country, winds abate, and daytime temperatures may climb above 32 degrees. Spring storms also bring moisture-laden air masses northwest across the plains from the Gulf of Mexico, pushing them up against the mountains. Some 40 percent of the east-slope moisture comes from such systems. This moisture falls as heavy, wet snows, which provide the essential water to initiate growth when temperatures rise.

PERIGLACIAL FEATURES

*A*lpine tundra in Rocky Mountain National Park is found primarily on surfaces that were above the reach of the Great Ice Age glaciers. These surfaces experienced a climate that was colder and wetter than the present one, and even today, the long, below-freezing winters cause the ground to become permanently frozen in places. A thin layer on top of this permafrost thaws during the short summer each year, creating three uniquely arctic/alpine surface features: patterned ground, solifluction terraces and frost hummocks.

These arctic-like features form in the thawed portion of the ground, where freezing and thawing cause repeated movement of the earth. In the alpine region of Rocky Mountain National Park, there are 88 crossings of the freezing point each year. This means that 88 times a year, water expands by 9 percent as it turns to ice and contracts again as it turns to water.

This powerful expansion/contraction process causes movement in loose material and sorts large rocks from finer materials. The result is the patterned ground so commonly found on the tundra – rocks concentrated into polygons, circles, streams, pavements and whole seas of jagged rock standing on edge. Rocks are thrust up through the ground by the frost action, and they eventually fall to add to the evolving patterns. In the Arctic, rocks have been thrust 45 feet skyward by the same process.

Masses of ice form and expand in wet areas, pushing up and out. This pressure causes solifluction, a slow, imperceptible downhill movement of the thawed material over the permanently frozen mass beneath. The result is either large terraces – often with pools – or lobed garlands. This action is less common today than during the Great Ice Age, but it still occurs in some places.

Isolated ice masses also elevate the ground above, making portions of the dense, wet turf form irregular columns called frost hummocks. Hundreds of square miles of these features cover Arctic landscapes, making ground travel very difficult.

THE SPREAD OF THE ALPINE TUNDRA

*T*undra plant communities look very much the same throughout the world, much more alike than the varieties of forest, grassland or desert systems. This similarity is attributable to two features: the parallel adaptations of plants to their environment and the large number of common plant species.

For example, 46 percent of the species found on Trail Ridge within Rocky Mountain National Park also grow in tundra sites around the Northern Hemisphere. Many species grow in Canada, Alaska and Siberia, and a significant number are distributed in Scandinavia. Some grow in both the Northern and Southern hemispheres, in places such as the Andes of South America and Africa's Mount Kilimanjaro. Just a few species of alpine tundra plants growing on Trail Ridge are found only in the Rocky Mountains. Collectively, alpine plants tell fascinating stories about the spread of life across the face of the Earth and adjustments to a most remarkable world.

Queens Crown
Rose Crown
Clementsia rhodantha
Stonecrop family

Both kings crown and closely related queens crown grace the tundra with their pinks and reds. These species have succulent leaves that aid in storing water. In the fall, these leaves may turn a brilliant red and orange. Kings crown is found in dry, gravelly areas, whereas queens crown inhabits boggy sites. Queens crown has pink flowers borne in cone-shaped flower clusters and a rib on the underside of each leaf. Kings crown has a flat-topped cluster of wine-red blossoms and leaves coated with a blue-white wax. The flowers of kings crown usually are unisexual, with male and female blossoms growing on different plants.

Kings Crown
Rhodiola integrifolia
Stonecrop family

The flattened clusters of deep-red flowers atop the kings crown appear in mid-summer. In September, the entire plant turns a brilliant coral-red color.

Alpine Lousewort

Pedicularis scopulorum
Snapdragon family

Restricted to wet tundra areas, the alpine lousewort is a rare find. Its odd-shaped blossoms are just the right size for bumblebees, and pollination occurs as bees scrape their backs against overhanging stigmas, the female receptive organs of the flowers. Louseworts were named by the English, who believed that cattle became infested with lice after they grazed on these plants.

Parry Clover

Trifolium parryi
Pea family

In addition to reproducing by seed, Parry clover can produce new plants by means of underground runners. The irregular shape and strong scent of this clover flower indicate that it is pollinated by bees. Flies, however, are much more common pollinators on the tundra. Flowers pollinated by flies tend to be less fragrant and usually have cup-shaped floral arrangements. All three clovers listed here grow only in the Rocky Mountains.

Pygmy Bitterroot

Oreobroma pygmaea
Purslane family

A relative of the Montana state flower, pygmy bitterroot is most commonly found in moist, gravelly areas in shallow snowbeds. It stores carbohydrates and nutrients in its large root, ensuring adequate growth during the short summer season. Unlike most alpine plants, its fleshy leaves grow first, followed by white, pink or fuchsia-colored flowers. The genus name is Greek for "mountain food" and refers to the somewhat edible quality of the bitter root.

Dwarf Clover

Trifolium nanum
Pea family

Millions of years of evolution produced this tough clover, one able to withstand winter's harshest winds in the high alpine fellfields. The large, spherical flower clusters normally associated with clovers have been reduced to a few short-stalked blossoms tucked into dense mats of tiny leaves. This slow-growing plant produces only a few serrated leaves each year, and mats 8 to 10 inches across may be more than 50 years old.

Alpine Clover
Trifolium dasyphyllum
Pea family

Two features distinguish alpine clover from Parry clover. Alpine clover has narrow, folded, sharp-tipped, bluish leaves and two-tone white and pink flowers. Parry clover has broader, greener leaves and larger flowers that are a more uniform deep-rose to wine color. Alpine clover forms large, dense carpets that stabilize the windblown soil in alpine fellfields. Parry clover grows in moist to wet sites, including shallow snowbeds. Clovers are among the few tundra plants that harbor nitrogen-fixing bacteria in their roots.

Alpine Primrose
Fairy Primrose
Primula angustifolia
Primrose family

Alpine primrose is most suitably named, for it is one of the first alpine flowers to brighten the tundra each spring. *Primula*, its genus name, is derived from the Latin word *primus*, which means first. Each alpine primrose plant usually has only one sweet-smelling blossom, with rich magenta petals radiating from a yellow eye. Many plants are connected by subsurface branches, and the scoop-shaped leaves help collect what little water falls each summer.

Moss Campion

Silene acaulis ssp. *subacaulescens*
Pink family

Moss campion is the archetype alpine cushion plant. Resembling a compressed pincushion, this species possesses the ideal form to survive winter gales on the open tundra. Winds flow over the cushion as they do over an airplane wing, while dirt, debris and moisture are caught in its dense tangle of leaves. Moss campion may retain its withered leaves for 50 years, resulting in a cushion composed of 80 percent dead material. Soil accumulates in this way, providing a fertile bed for invading plants that eventually replace the cushion.

Alplily

Lloydia serotina
Lily family

This diminutive lily has long, narrow, succulent leaves and usually, only one cream-colored flower. Like many other lilies, it grows from a small bulb and often spreads by way of underground stems. A row of alplilies, for example, often can be found growing from the same root system along the base of a rock. This species grows in alpine habitats around the Northern Hemisphere.

Arctic Gentian

Gentianodes algida
Gentian family

The elegant blossoms of arctic gentian scattered throughout the meadow turf community signal the end of the brief alpine summer. This gentian is one of the last plants to bloom on the tundra, and as its name implies, it is also found throughout the Arctic. The purplish flower buds unfold into a vase-shaped white cup streaked and dotted with purple.

Black-headed Daisy

Erigeron melanocephalus
Sunflower family

The name black-headed daisy seems to contradict this plant's appearance. The term, however, refers to dark-purple hairs under the flower head that cover purple-green bracts. These daisies are usually found in the moist soil where late-lying snowbanks melt away. Their growing season, consequently, may be as short as four weeks.

White Marsh-marigold

Psychrophila leptosepala
Hellebore family

True to the temperature of the water where it lives, the genus name for marsh-marigold means "frigid-loving." Marsh-marigold grows mainly around the edges of tundra pools and other wet areas, and like the snow butter-cup, its flower can burst through the edge of melting snowbanks. Unlike other local species with which it can be confused, it has large, basal, heart-shaped leaves that are not divided. The word marigold is thought to be a contraction of "Mary's gold," a name given to this plant's many gold-hued relatives found throughout the world.

Globeflower

Trollius albiflorus
Hellebore family

Although mainly a subalpine plant, globeflower is sometimes found in moist tundra areas, especially in the myriad rivulets below melting snowbanks near treelimit. Globeflower is distinguished from similar-looking alpine plants by its hairless, lobed leaves that surround the flower stem, with each lobe serrated or toothed. In contrast to the pure white of marsh-marigold, the globeflower blossom is yellowish at first, later fading to a creamy white.

Mountain Dryad

Dryas octopetala ssp. *hookeriana*
Rose family

This alpine plant with large white flowers is sometimes confused with marsh-marigold, globeflower and narcissus anemone, but in contrast to these, its flowers have eight petals. It usually grows on exposed, gravelly alpine ridges, and the soil beneath it is often high in calcium or has a limestone base. Dryads are, in fact, low-growing shrubs with crinkly evergreen leaves and woody stems. When ripe, the seed heads resemble white-haired waifs waiting to be carried away to distant lands.

Narcissus Anemone
Alpine Anemone

Anemonastrum narcissiflorum ssp. *zephyrum*
Buttercup family

The Greeks believed anemones grew wherever Venus' tears fell to earth. This lovely plant usually has three flowers growing from the tip of the same stem. The foliage is covered with long, wispy hairs, and each flower cluster has a whorl of leaf-like bracts below it.

Big-rooted Springbeauty
Alpine Springbeauty

Claytonia megarhiza
Purslane family

This alpine species has rosettes of large, spatulate, fleshy leaves surrounded by a ring of pinkish-white blossoms. A single root, as thick as a large carrot and 6 feet or more in length, enables the plant to find moisture in even the driest tundra soils. Springbeauty grows in rocky and gravelly areas.

Snowball Saxifrage

Micranthes rhomboidea
Saxifrage family

While blooming, this plant's flower cluster resembles a miniature snowball. And like many other saxifrages, its blossoms are perched upon a slender stem growing from a rosette of wide, slightly fleshy, diamond-shaped leaves. The word saxifrage means "rock breaker." It refers either to the family's habit of growing in rock crevices, or to an ancient medicinal use for breaking kidney stones. This belief was attributed more to the kidney-shaped leaves of some species than to their medicinal value.

Alpine Bistort

Bistorta vivipara
Buckwheat family

Many plants have evolved ways to circumvent the short alpine growing season. As the species name *vivipara* implies, this plant bears its offspring live without going through the flower-to-seed process. Tiny bulblets form on the flower stalk below the flowers, and when one leaf unfurls, the whole bulblet drops off to establish itself the same season. Alpine bistort seeds have never been known to germinate in the Rocky Mountains.

American Bistort

Bistorta bistortoides
Buckwheat family

One of the more visible and taller plants on the alpine tundra, American bistort bobs and sways on its slender red stem in the slightest breeze. This movement poses a considerable challenge to even the most patient photographer. Ptarmigan feed on the flower heads by pecking at them with vigor. Naturalists have nicknamed the bistort "dirty socks," as some of the plants have a distinctly unpleasant aroma. Some flower heads may turn pinkish with age, making them look like their near relatives growing in the Alps.

Snowlover

Chionophila jamesii
Snapdragon family

Found only in the Rocky Mountains, this little plant thrives in snow accumulation areas. Its long creamy-white blossoms are always found growing on one side of the plant, and the leaves turn a brownish-black color after drying. Its species name, *jamesii*, honors Edwin James, botanist and geologist on an 1820 expedition into the West. The genus name is Greek for "snow lover."

Dotted Saxifrage
Ciliaria austromontana
Saxifrage family

Looking as though they contracted a case of the measles, the petals of this saxifrage are speckled with orange and magenta dots. The plant's spine-tipped leaves – resembling those of juniper – form small rosettes. Dotted saxifrage forms extensive mats throughout all life zones in the Rocky Mountains.

Alpine Sandwort
Lidia obtusiloba
Chickweed family

Also known as sandywinks, alpine sandworts thrive in windswept, snow-free areas, forming large, compact mats of tiny leaves attached to large root systems. The blossoms seem huge, almost out-of-place, when compared to the leaves. There are, however, two distinct petal sizes. Male flowers have large petals, whereas the female petals are much reduced in size.

Mountain Candytuft
Noccaea montana
Mustard family

Mountain candytuft blooms very early in the alpine tundra, allowing quick pollination before many of the surrounding species produce flowers. This relative of pennycress often bears a number of flat and compact floral rosettes, which grow from a common stalk. Its leaves are coated with a whitish powder.

Fendler Sandwort

Eremogone fendleri
Chickweed family

At first glance, the petals of the Fendler sandwort appear to have a large red dot in their centers. Closer inspection reveals that the dots are actually stamens, the male reproductive parts of the flower. After the stamens wither and fall off with age, the petals resume their white appearance. Named for the botanist August Fendler, this sandwort has long, grass-like leaves.

Northern Rockjasmine

Androsace septentrionalis
Primrose family

This member of the primrose family has a yellow center, which is believed to guide pollinating insects to its nectaries. Rockjasmine petals are almost rectangular in shape, and each blossom is perched on top of a pedicle, or stalk. In the tundra, these pedicles are very short. Look for the star-like flowers in areas disturbed by pocket gophers and meadow voles.

Koenigia

Koenigia islandica
Buckwheat family

Koenigia is the park's only annual alpine plant. Named for Swiss botanist Emmanuel Koenig, this minute buckwheat grows from seed and produces new seed in the same season. Nearly all other tundra species – more than 330 in Colorado alone – are perennials, which develop over a period of years. Koenigia grows in wet, gravelly areas and moss banks where temperatures never exceed 46 degrees.

Rydbergia Alpine Sunflower

Rydbergia grandiflora
Sunflower family

Rydbergia is a giant among Rocky Mountain alpine plants. Its nickname, "old-man-of-the-mountain," refers to the dense hair covering its foliage. This hair diffuses strong ultraviolet radiation, traps heat and reduces water loss. The flower heads usually face east, away from the prevailing wind. Each plant stores food over a several-year period until it has sufficient nutrients and energy to blossom. After the seed matures, the plant dies. Rydbergia is one of the few alpine plants endemic to the Rockies.

Snow Lily Avalanche Lily Glacier Lily

Erythronium grandiflorum
Lily family

Gracing both subalpine and lower-alpine snowbed areas, this beautiful lily truly is a snow lover. It blooms as snowbanks recede up the mountainsides in places such as Wild Basin and the western slopes of the park. Native Americans ate the greens and dug bulbs for food, but the plant now is protected by law for all to enjoy. Hungry bears and other wildlife are excepted from the rule.

Gold Flower

Tetraneuris brevifolia
Sunflower family

Gold flower, or little alpine sunflower, grows in gravelly areas, sometimes near its larger relative, Rydbergia. The two species are easily distinguished by their leaves – gold flower has small, simple leaves, whereas the Rydbergia's foliage is deeply dissected. Gold flower grows both in the foothills and on the tundra, skipping the montane and subalpine life zones.

Western Yellow Paintbrush

Castilleja occidentalis
Snapdragon family

The splashes of light yellow these plants add to the tundra are provided by the flowers' leafy bracts and sepals – not their hidden green petals. A second (and uncommon) yellow species, the alpine paintbrush, grows at higher elevations and has pinnately divided upper leaves. Many paintbrushes at lower elevations parasitize nearby sage plants to draw nutrients from them. This may not be true for the alpine species.

Snow Buttercup

Ranunculus adoneus
Buttercup family

A snowbank may seem like a cold environment for a flower, but the hardy blossoms of snow buttercup have been found partially open under 12 feet of snow in the middle of winter. Insulation is the key. Temperatures rarely drop below 26 degrees more than 2 feet below the snow surface, but winter temperatures in the alpine air may plunge to -35. In summer, look for the ruffled, shiny yellow petals and finely divided foliage near snowbanks. This species is native to the Rockies.

Alpine Avens

Acomastylis rossii ssp. *turbinata*
Rose family

This yellow rose of the tundra is an important member of turf communities and gopher gardens. It is one of the more abundant alpine wildflowers in the Rockies. The finely dissected, fern-like leaves contain high quantities of anthocyanin – antifreeze-like pigments that can convert sunlight to heat. The pigments also serve as sunscreens to filter out ultraviolet radiation. As fall approaches and the green chlorophyll pigments decompose, the anthocyanin shines forth, painting the tundra in brilliant hues of deep ruby red.

Western Wallflower

Erysimum capitatum
Mustard family

This plant's powerful fragrance attracts bees and people alike. One family name, Cruciferae, refers to the four petals arranged at right angles, forming cross-shaped flowers that brighten snow-free tundra slopes each spring. Some alpine wallflowers have lilac-to-purple blossoms. Regardless of the color, the blossoms open early to attract pollinators before the stems reach their full height.

Goldbloom Saxifrage

Hirculus serpyllifolius ssp.
chrysanthus
Saxifrage family

The goldbloom's miniature rosettes of shiny leaves (smaller than fingernails) often are found in gravelly areas on rocky ridges. Each rosette resembles a classic Chinese chrysanthemum. The brilliant, golden-yellow petals are spotted with red-orange, and after pollination, the seed pods turn a bright red. Unlike whiplash saxifrage, goldbloom saxifrage does not have runners or hairs.

Whiplash Saxifrage

Hirculus platysepalus ssp. *crandallii*
Saxifrage family

Barren frost boils and other gravelly areas are quickly invaded by this pioneering species. Each plant sends out thread-like runners (whiplashes) with tiny plants at the end, similar to those of the strawberry. After the new plant takes root, the runners wither and the process is repeated. The stems and leaf edges are covered with minute translucent and glandular hairs.

Yellow Stonecrop

Amerosedum lanceolatum
Stonecrop family

The stonecrop is perfectly suited to grow among the rocks, where it blooms in late summer. Fat, succulent, wax-coated leaves retain water, while a thicker, gelatin-like sap is stored in many of the plant's interior cells. These adaptations allow stonecrop to live at all elevations, from low deserts to the windy, dry, snow-free areas of the alpine tundra. Some members of this family are hardy enough that botanists must destroy the epidermal layers to keep picked specimens from growing – even after they have been pressed.

Sibbaldia Cloverleaf Rose

Sibbaldia procumbens
Rose family

Named for a Scottish botanist, this tiny member of the rose family is sometimes mistaken for a clover. Each leaflet of the Sibbaldia, however, has three distinct points. Because this species always grows in areas where snowfields stay late into the summer, Scandinavians use it as an indicator of where not to build their roads.

Alpine Parsley

Oreoxis alpina
Parsley family

The leaves of alpine parsley grow from large taproots in mature, dry turfs. Its blossom is composed of tiny individual flowers, with each petal the size of a pinhead. Collectively, the petals can support the weight of a fly, whose abdomen is dusted with pollen each time it flies from one flower head to another. Like some other members of the parsley family, the alpine parsley has finely divided leaves.

Drabas

Draba spp.
Mustard family

Several draba species grow on the tundra, ranging in size from small to infinitesimal. These different mustard species are difficult, at times, to distinguish. The spiral-shaped seeds of the twisted-pod draba, however, make it easy to identify. Drabas add a dash of yellow or white to the tundra mosaic in many dry alpine meadows and disturbed sites.

Colorado Columbine

Aquilegia coerulea
Hellebore family

This beautiful plant derives its name from the Latin word *columba*, meaning dove; its long spurs and petals were thought to resemble a circle of doves dancing around the stem. Native Americans used a tea made from the seeds to cure headaches and fevers, and Europeans once believed members of this genus were effective in combating plague. In the early days of tourism, the columbine was nearly eradicated by collectors. The plant now is protected throughout Colorado. At higher altitudes, a shorter, compact form of Colorado columbine can be found growing in rock piles and other sheltered areas.

Dwarf Columbine
Alpine Columbine

Aquilegia saximontana
Hellebore family

This pint-sized relative of the Colorado columbine is a rare find. It usually grows in the shade of alpine nooks and crannies beneath overhanging rocks, and is readily distinguished from its sister species by the hooked spurs on the flowers. These small spurs contain nectar, which attracts pollinators to the flower. The ephemeral petals quickly drop off, making the dwarf columbine even harder to find in late summer. Most believe the genus name, *Aquilegia*, refers to "water collector."

Pinnateleaf Daisy

Erigeron pinnatisectus
Sunflower family

Many species of daisies grow on the tundra in Colorado. Like other sunflowers, or composites, their blossoms are composed of hundreds of individual flowers packed into heads that resemble single flowers. The word daisy originally came from the Anglo-Saxon "day's eye," referring to a flower that opened at sunrise and closed as the sun set. The leaves of the pinnateleaf daisy are deeply divided into thin lobes. It grows in snow-free areas.

Alpine Kittentail

Besseya alpina
Snapdragon family

Alpine kittentail's small tuft of purple flowers only can be found in the alpine tundra. The plants grow among rocks and bloom in early spring. This species, however, sometimes is confused with purple fringe, a larger

plant that normally grows at lower elevations. Alpine kittentails have oval leaves with serrated edges, whereas the leaves of purple fringe are deeply divided, fern-like and silver-gray. The dense cluster of flowers no doubt reminded the naming botanist of a kitten's tail.

Sky Pilot

Polemonium viscosum
Phlox family

The sky-blue, deep-blue or occasional white blossoms of sky pilot grow high in the Rockies wherever tundra has been disturbed by pocket gophers or humans. The species name, *viscosum*, refers to sticky glands that produce the odor from which the plant derives its less-appealing name, skunkweed. Sky pilots found near treelimit smell much more skunk-like than plants growing at higher elevations. Apparently, the odor repels nectar-stealing ants, which are more common at lower elevations.

Greenleaf Chiming Bells

Mertensia lanceolata
Borage family

Greenleaf chiming bells grows in stable turfs and fellfields. Like sky pilot, it quickly colonizes disturbed sites. At lower elevations, the plants grow in pine forests and open, dry areas. The beautiful sky-blue flowers hang down, protecting the flower pollen from rain and hail. The rare alpine chiming bells is a close relative, and it may hybridize with greenleaf chiming bells. The family name, Borage, refers to the woolly foliage many of its species possess.

Alpine Harebell
One-flowered Harebell

Campanula uniflora
Bellflower family

The tiny steel-blue flowers of the alpine harebell attract the smallest of pollinating insects. This plant has deeply notched blossoms and is found in dry, turfy areas of the tundra, whereas mountain harebell grows in disturbed or gravelly sites. Harebells are eaten by many animals, including pikas, marmots, deer, elk, sheep and bears. They were also used by the Cheyenne Indians for a religious ceremony.

Mountain Harebell

Campanula rotundifolia
Bellflower family

"... as if like snow flowers they had fallen from the sky; and, though frail and delicate-looking none of its companions is more enduring or rings out the praise of beauty-loving Nature in tones more appreciable to mortals."
— John Muir

Mountain harebells grace the mountains from the foothills to the lower areas of the alpine tundra. This same plant is the bluebell of Scotland, and it is found around the world in the Northern Hemisphere. The bright-blue petals of the blossom are united and shallowly lobed; the upper leaves on the stem are linear. On the tundra, the blossoms often appear large, for the leaves and stems are reduced in size.

Alpine Forget-me-not

Eritrichum aretioides
Borage family

Casual explorers and mountaineers alike delight in the fragrance of this early bloomer. Most of these plants have deep-blue blossoms with yellow, nectar-guiding centers, but an occasional white-flowered plant also may be found. The leaves of this plant are covered with long, soft, heat-retaining hairs, and appropriately, the genus name means "woolly hair." Many tales are attached to the forget-me-not name. These range from stories of beautiful maidens who longed to be remembered forever to bitter memories of the leaf's taste.

Moss Gentian

Chondrophylla prostrata
Gentian family

This tiny flower must be carefully searched for, as passing shadows cause the petals to close – often for several hours. This adaptation prevents raindrops the size of the blossom from washing away the pollen. Gentians were named for King Gentius of ancient Illyria, who discovered their medicinal value. This species has an alpine distribution in both the Northern and Southern hemispheres.

Alpine Phlox

Phlox sibirica ssp. *pulvinata*
Phlox family

At times, the blossoms of the phlox are so abundant they cover the entire plant. The pale-blue or white petals of the fragile-looking flowers belie the harsh fellfield environment where this cushion plant thrives. The genus name, *phlox*, comes from the Greek word for flame or fire. Its subspecies name, *pulvinata*, refers to the plant's cushion shape.

Alpine Alumroot

Heuchera parvifolia var. *nivalis*
Saxifrage family

Like a number of other alpine plants, the alumroot of the tundra is a miniature version of the same species found at lower elevations. This saxifrage grows in rock crevices and can form carpets over barren scree slopes. Its seemingly green flowers are, in fact, yellow. Many alumroot leaves brighten the tundra each fall, when they turn a rose to wine red.

Thistles

Cirsium spp.
Sunflower family

Many thistles are noxious weeds that invade existing plant communities. The alpine thistles also are pioneering plants, but they are native. These species commonly are found along

roadsides and in other disturbed areas at high elevations. In time, as the soil develops, they will be succeeded by more familiar alpine plants. Thistles look totally out-of-place in the tundra, where they tower above their ankle-high neighbors.

Willows

Salix spp.
Willow family

At least four species of willows grow in tundra areas. The arctic willow, with long, grayish leaves, and the round-leaved snow willow form large carpets close to the ground. The other two species

are bush-like. In reality, the flowers of willows are a dingy brown. White-tailed ptarmigan, ground-dwelling alpine birds, actually can gain weight through the winter by feeding on willow buds. One ounce of oven-dried buds may contain as many as 112,000 calories.

Alpine Sorrel

Oxyria digyna
Buckwheat family

One of the more widely distributed and studied tundra species, alpine sorrel can be found growing along roadsides and in other gravelly spots. Sorrel leaves were eaten by Eskimos and Arctic explorers for their high vitamin C content, and animals often graze on the plants. Sorrel comes from an old German word for sour; *oxys* means sour in Greek. Look closely. Its tiny flowers are, in fact, white.

Sageworts
Artemisia spp.
Sunflower family

Four species of sage are found on the alpine tundra, including the fringed sagewort depicted here. Rocky Mountain sagewort is one of the more common plants in the tundra, and its gray-green, finely divided leaves can be seen in most tundra ecosystems. The drab-looking, yellowish flowers are composed of dozens of minute blossoms packed into each head. These flowers are mainly pollinated by the wind and lack the large, colorful petals of most plants that attract insects.

Alpine Nailwort
Paronychia pulvinata
Chickweed family

The tiny, leathery leaves and yellow-green flowers of this cushion plant are much hardier than they first may appear. Nailworts can grow over bare rock, and their thick, woody roots penetrate deep into the ground. Both the genus and the common name indicate this plant was once used to cure a disease of the fingernails.

	Page Number	MAY	JUNE	JULY	AUGUST	SEPTEMBER	ALPINE TURFS	FELLFIELDS	SNOWBEDS	WET MEADOWS	GOPHER GARDENS	ROCK/GRAVEL AREAS	RESTRICTED TO COLORADO	RESTRICTED TO ROCKY MOUNTAINS	MOUNTAINS OF WESTERN NORTH AMERICA	NORTH AMERICAN ARCTIC AND ALPINE	NORTHERN HEMISPHERE ARCTIC AND ALPINE	NORTHERN AND SOUTHERN HEMISPHERES
Alpine alumroot	34			■								■						
Alpine avens	26		■	■	■		■	■			■					■		
Alpine bistort	21			■	■												■	
Alpine clover	15			■				■						■				
Alpine forget-me-not	33		■	■			■										■	
Alpine harebell / One-flowered harebell	32			■	■												■	
Alpine kittentail	30	■	■									■		■				
Alpine lousewort	13				■													
Alpine nailwort	36		■					■										
Alpine parsley	28		■	■			■											
Alpine phlox	33			■												■		
Alpine primrose / Fairy primrose	15	■	■				■							■				
Alpine sandwort	22		■	■												■		
Alpine sorrel	35			■	■							■						■
Alplily	17		■	■														
American bistort	21			■	■		■	■		■						■		
Arctic gentian	17				■													
Big-rooted springbeauty / Alpine springbeauty	20			■				■			■	■				■		
Black-headed daisy	18			■	■				■	■					■			
Colorado columbine	29			■								■	■					

37

	Page Number	ALPINE TUNDRA BLOOM PERIODS					TUNDRA ECOSYSTEMS						DISTRIBUTION					
		May	June	July	August	September	Alpine Turfs	Fellfields	Snowbeds	Wet Meadows	Gopher Gardens	Rock/Gravel Areas	Restricted to Colorado	Restricted to Rocky Mountains	Mountains of Western North America	North American Arctic and Alpine	Northern Hemisphere Arctic and Alpine	Northern and Southern Hemispheres
Dotted saxifrage	22			●								●			●		●	
Drabas	28		●	●			●		●				VARIABLE BY SPECIES					
Dwarf clover	14		●												●			
Dwarf columbine Alpine columbine	29			●								●		●				
Fendler sandwort	23			●											●			
Globeflower	19			●						●							●	
Goldbloom saxifrage	27			●			●					●					●	
Gold flower	25			●			●								●			
Greenleaf chiming bells	31			●			●		●	●					●			
Kings crown	12			●	●				●	●							●	
Koenigia	23			●					●	●								●
Moss campion	16			●			●	●									●	
Moss gentian	33			●						●								●
Mountain candytuft	22		●				●				●						●	
Mountain dryad	19			●				●									●	
Mountain harebell	32				●							●					●	
Narcissus anemone Alpine anemone	20			●			●		●								●	
Northern rockjasmine	23	●	●					●			●						●	
Parry clover	13			●						●				●				
Pinnateleaf daisy	30			●											●			

38

ALPINE TUNDRA
BLOOM PERIODS   TUNDRA
ECOSYSTEMS   DISTRIBUTION

	Page Number	May	June	July	August	September	Alpine Turfs	Fellfields	Snowbeds	Wet Meadows	Gopher Gardens	Rock/Gravel Areas	Restricted to Colorado	Restricted to Rocky Mountains	Mountains of Western North America	North American Arctic and Alpine	Northern Hemisphere Arctic and Alpine	Northern and Southern Hemispheres
Pygmy bitterroot	14			■					■					■				
Queens crown / Rose crown	12			■	■					■				■				
Rydbergia / Alpine sunflower	24			■			■	■						■				
Sageworts	36			■	■		■	■					VARIABLE BY SPECIES					
Sibbaldia / Cloverleaf rose	28			■	■		■		■								■	
Sky pilot	31			■				■			■	■		■				
Snowball saxifrage	20		■				■							■				
Snow buttercup	25		■						■					■				
Snow lily/Avalanche lily / Glacier lily	24	■	■						■						■			■
Snowlover	21	■	■						■						■			
Thistles	34			■	■							■	VARIABLE BY SPECIES					
Western wallflower	26		■				■								■			
Western yellow paintbrush	25			■	■										■			
Whiplash saxifrage	27		■	■			■								■			
White marsh-marigold	18		■	■					■						■			
Willows	35		■	■			■			■			VARIABLE BY SPECIES					
Yellow stonecrop	27			■	■		■	■			■							

■ Average bloom periods

▨ Year-to-year bloom variations

"The loveliest flowers are those that cling closest to the earth."
— John Keble

ABOUT THE AUTHORS

Beatrice E. (Bettie) Willard (1925-2003) was one of the nation's leading specialists in alpine tundra ecology. She had intimate knowledge of the tundra communities of Rocky Mountain National Park gained through more than a quarter century of field work. She also had experience with the alpine regions of Europe and Alaska. Willard was co-author of the classic book *Land Above the Trees* and was a professor at the Colorado School of Mines, where she created and served as head of the environmental sciences and engineering ecology department.

Michael Smithson was a district naturalist at Rocky Mountain National Park, where he worked for many years with special emphasis on interpreting the alpine tundra. He is a professional photographer and author of *Rocky Mountain – The Story Behind the Scenery*.

REVISION PROJECT COORDINATOR – JOHN GUNN

BOOK DESIGN – ANN GREEN

EDITORIAL REVIEW – LEANNE BENTON

ILLUSTRATIONS – WENDY SMITH

PHOTOGRAPHIC ACKNOWLEDGMENTS –

DUANE B. SQUIRES: INSIDE FRONT COVER, INSIDE BACK COVER, BACK COVER, 1, 12-1, 12-2, 13-1, 14-1, 14-2, 15-1, 15-2, 16, 17-2, 18-2, 19-2, 22-2, 24-1, 24-2, 25-2, 25-3, 26-2, 27-3, 29-1, 31-1, 32-2, 33-1, 33-3

ROCKY MOUNTAIN NATIONAL PARK: 17-1, 18-1, 20-2, 20-3, 21-1, 21-2, 21-3, 22-1, 26-1, 28-3, 29-2, 36-1, 36-2

LEANNE BENTON: 23-2, 27-1, 27-2, 28-1, 28-2, 30-1, 30-2, 32-1, 33-2, 35-1

LINDA AND RICHARD BEIDLEMAN: 13-2, 22-3, 23-1, 25-1, 31-2, 34-1

DENVER BOTANIC GARDENS: 19-1, 20-1, 34-2, 35-2

GLENN RANDALL: FRONT COVER, 2

LORAINE YEATTS: 23-3

MARY ANN KRESSIG: 5

(*Back cover photos, clockwise from top left*)
Alplily, sky pilot, alpine primrose and snow lily